GRANNIE BLOCK

BALBOA
PRESS
A DIVISION OF HAY HOUSE

Balboa Press books may be ordered through booksellers or by contacting:

Balboa Press
A Division of Hay House
1663 Liberty Drive
Bloomington, IN 47403
www.balboapress.com
1 (877) 407-4847

ISBN: 978-1-9822-2087-7 (sc)
ISBN: 978-1-9822-2088-4 (e)

Print information available on the last page.

Balboa Press rev. date: 02/01/2019

Dear Love Ones,

I shared with a well known published author that I wanted to write a book for my grandchildren and all the great greats to follow. The author asked me, "What was the message I wanted to share?"

My response was quick, yet reflective of her comment. " I do not really have a strong opinion about the purpose. I just know the audience I want to address." My new mentor shared, "You will know when it comes."

It was not really clear in my mind as to just what the writing would look like. Would it be a series of educational books titled, "What's in Grannie's Red Bag? (The red bag has been with me everywhere I continued to go since visiting Michael in New York City 19 years ago.)

I then dismissed my first idea. Thinking about my new mentor's words, the desire to share something on a deeper, more important level to all of you became stronger.

Today, August 15, 2017, a year later, I have a clearer vision of the message as well as the design of the book. And so, to my dear buddy, I say with such gratitude for your wisdom, "You were so correct. I do now know my message!"

My message to you was really influenced by something that left a lifelong impression on me.

My Dad died when he was only 29, I was seven, and my sister Judie was 2 ½. To say we did not really know much about this wonderful man that everyone seemed to love and admire is an understatement.

In those days, I guess people felt they were protecting his children by never speaking about the tragedy.

One of the very few pictures I have of Daddy is from his bar mitzvah. Before my very own Bat Mitzvah ceremony at age 60, I just happened to remove that picture from the frame. Behind the glass was his handwritten speech he gave on that important day. Feeling a sense of awe in that I had something from Daddy, in his own handwriting, sharing personal feelings, was beyond a memorable moment for me. I was so grateful to learn even that little bit about him-even though it was just thoughts on his 8 by 10 notebook paper. My Dad's several statements spoke to me in many significant ways and led me to choose my sermon's theme, "Who is Bonnie Block?"

Today, fifteen years later, I am grateful to be Grannie to you-my five most outstanding and wonderful grandchildren -Jordan, Yale, Benjamin, Ellie, and Nora. Having stories that others will tell about your grandmother in years to come (Please God let there be many) will be great. Yet, I want you to have more than those comments, and more than messages on a lined school paper, to know your "Grannie"

My passion for writing this book became a way for me to talk personally to you, my grandchildren, and all the great greats to follow. My hope is that you will hear Grannie's voice thru your readings and find the messages useful and inspiring on your life's journey. I give these to you my dear ones with so much love and forever hugs.

Love,

Grannie

xoxoxo

My favorite quote is...

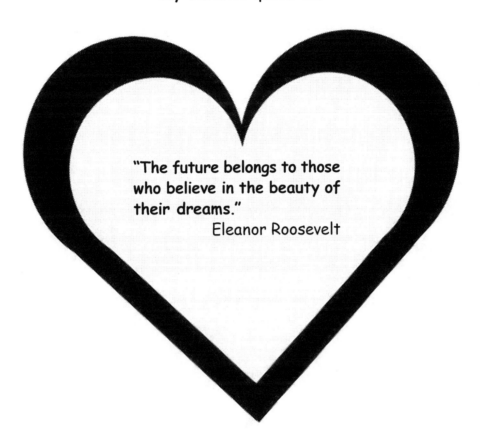

"The future belongs to those who believe in the beauty of their dreams."
Eleanor Roosevelt

I have been called a dreamer, a "what if "person, a person who plants golden seeds, a person who is committed to being a positive hope salesman in every opportunity, a person who is most grateful, and one who recognizes that she is so very blessed.

Children, may you all become dreamers, and go forth to discover and fulfill your dreams. I feel certain that each of you have been given the gifts to reach success in whatever goals you choose throughout your life's journey.

"You can if you think you can!"

Love,
Grannie
xoxoxo

In 1987, I drove to Richmond to visit a friend I met at a conference in California. Both events, even now, seem unimaginable. Why never before had I driven alone for that long until…

Six years ago, we purchased a wonderful beach home. Two years ago, I was going to have the amazing opportunity to spend the entire summer there. Super great! One big problem became apparent. How was my car getting there? Me? Drive alone for 2 hours and 40 minutes? Cross that Bay Bridge? YIKES!

I needed a plan. I wrote "Yes I Can!" on colored paper and placed it on my passenger seat in full view. Pop led the way in his car. Repeating my mantra," Yes I Can! " I placed the key in the ignition and off I went! The first part of the drive went smoothly. Then came that bridge. I held my anchor tightly all the way over those 4 miles, repeating -well-you know what! And I did it! The rest of the way was super great! I have accomplished this major feat several times now, still using my anchor. Most times, I add, "Thank You God! " I do feel very proud!

My lesson was in the realization of how a difficult challenge becomes easier when you believe in yourself. I encourage you to look for ways to work thru your challenges. Most times, you will be in awe of all your skills you already have and some that some that come as a surprise!

"Plant golden seeds"

Love,
Grannie
xoxoxo

At times, seemingly out of nowhere, I become excited about an idea or project. I share it which then puts my thoughts out in the universe. Often, it comes to fruition, maybe not always matching the way I originally envisioned it or the timeline. I feel excited to have just done the planting.

Here is one that continues to bloom as I write. Thursday mornings are our parent workshops. Claudia, a Spanish mom, and her buddies, used to attend even though their English was limited. Unfortunately, due to changes in some immigrant policies, everyone but Claudia stopped coming. At the end of our last workshop for 2016-2017, I approached her with this idea. "What do you think about inviting friends to your home and I will bring the talks to you?" Quickly she responded. "I will make the coffee!" Just as quickly, I exclaimed, "Great! I will bring the doughnuts!"

We did and Familias has now been blossoming for two years. Claudia and Lillian have opened up their homes for the sharing of helpful information to help everyone reach personal and academic success. One of the guests does the translation.

We have truly become a family. It has been a great sense of pride and joy to have these wonderful people in my life.

"Help others recognize and embrace their special gifts"

Love,
Grannie
xoxoxo

Riverview Elementary every year hosts a school wide talent show where children and family members are the stars. Everyone becomes so very excited about this fun event. This particular year, Charles wanted to be part of the program. He attended the first rehearsal with his mom who shared, "He will sing, "I will always love you" by Whitney Houston. There was no music to be played or any kind of accompaniment for his performance.

I grew anxious as to how supportive "would be stars" would act during his tryout. You see, Charles had different abilities due to his Cerebral Palsy.

Not a problem! My Riverview angels were silent with respect and admiration as an angel began to sing. Charles was just amazing and at the end, the children all stood up giving him a standing ovation.

From show time on, whenever anyone saw him in the halls, you could hear, "Hi Charles" and Charles would respond back by placing this most beautiful smile on his face. He had truly become the shiniest star and taught everyone a lesson. Each of us has special gifts. Sometimes, they just need an opportunity and a little help to become unwrapped!

"Find a way to help make a difference in other people's lives"

Love,
Grannie
xoxoxo

♥ A kindergarten teacher shouted, "Mrs. Block, there is a child in my class who a horrendous infection throughout her mouth!" There was a dentist close to school so I grabbed my coat and went to go find help. After the office manager shared my story with the dentist, he agreed for her to come after school. Upon his exam, the doctor quickly contacted one of his classmates whose practice dealt with pediatric emergencies. "We can't let her die?" he stated to me.

The great news is that she was seen almost immediately by the specialist. She had 4 teeth removed, was given medicine for the infection, and had several follow up appointments to ensure the problem was gone. That was last year.

Since that time, the dear child has always gotten so excited to see me in the halls of our building. She will quickly get out of line to give me a hug. I tell her I love her and smiling, she returns to be with her class. Last week, the same routine occurred. This day, she had a bracelet in her hand. I could tell she thought a lot about this piece of jewelry. I commented, "That is so pretty!" "That is my mommy's and she gave it to me" she shared ever so proudly. "Oh my, it is so beautiful." With that, she gave me the bracelet. "I want you to have it." She expressed. "On no, mommy gave it to you." The dialogue continued. The child, "I want you to have it because you helped mommy help me to feel better." I did not know what to say or do. I knew I was going to find a way to return it.

After a few days passed, I went to see her. "I loved wearing your bracelet. Everyone thought it was so beautiful. Now I want to give it back to you. Remember, there are always ways to help someone and there is always someone to help you." She smiled, hugged me, I told her I loved her and off she went to class.

"Make time to relax in ways YOU enjoy, not by how others define, "Relaxing."

Love,
Grannie
xoxoxo

Today it is six degrees outside. The wind chill is due to go to two degrees this evening. People are complaining about everything, I am having a great, relaxing day. I did my yoga, read my prayerful affirmations, did a little ironing, a little redecorating, spent 30 minutes on the treadmill, listened to great music, read several chapters from a good book, meditated, and now I am working on my beloved writing project.

My Julie called as I was writing this story to share about her great relaxing day. "Mom, I had such a fun time today! I baked, painted, worked on puzzles, knitted, sewed, and played games. I just love this kind of day!" Many people do not think what my daughter and I did could provide relaxation. "Bonnie, Don't you ever just sit and relax?" Sometimes I just smile and that is my answer. Sometimes I will share one or two of the above activities I enjoy. Why, I might also be writing about a moment of time for my journal, working on a house or school project, knitting, or in better weather, walking for two miles and/or gardening.

I feel so grateful and blessed that I have so many wonderful ways I can choose to unwind. It is all about me! Dear love ones, define your own way for relaxing. Remember, it is all about you!

"Hug yourself often throughout your day...really throughout all your years."

Love,
Grannie
xoxoxo

♥ Throughout your life's journey, reflect and praise yourself often, as if you were talking to a beloved young child.

The size of your effort and/or accomplishment is not a measure for when you will give yourself such positive sentiments. Feeding your body positive affirmations feeds your soul and enhances the quality of your life.

Please remember loving yourself is a gift to yourself that also enables you to then love others.

What would your hug look like?

That is for you to determine.

For me, it may be spending time with family, a hot fudge sundae, shopping, working with flowers, etc. Cooking is not on my list of hugs-that is Pop's favorite and I am his grateful cheerleader!

"Keep moving forward at your own pace, regardless of the stones, hills, or mountains you may have to overcome."

Love,
Grannie
xoxoxo

♥ I did not really want to retire from teaching. The school system changed the focus of family involvement. My successful curriculum for this important component of any school was to be eliminated. Standing firm on my beliefs, I put in my resignation. I kept saying to myself and to others when asked, "I want to just renaissance myself in some fashion, in some way, that will continue to help caregivers help their children." How? Where? When? What do I do next? These were my constant inner thoughts for which I had no answers.

This was the unchartered path that I followed to get to the top of my mountain.

Pop and I volunteered in the Israeli Army. We came home, went to the beach and late summer my sister was diagnosed with breast cancer. Six months later, I was told the same news as Judie. After my radiation treatments, Mary Maddox, my former classroom parent, who Pop and I helped fulfill a dream of becoming a teacher, became a Principal. First, I volunteered with her for a year and then, for three years, worked in her school two days a week, doing many things, including my parent business program.

Mary M and now Mary P and I have been working together for seven awesome years in the school where I left my heart, Riverview. I am grateful and proud to share that I am doing my family and business programs that are more successful than I could ever imagine. It was not easy. I just kept believing, and becoming engaged in ways that had the possibility of moving up the mountain to reach my goal. I am sitting now on top of my mountain and loving life!

"Passion +Commitment +Perseverance =Success"

"Be proud and grateful for all the gifts you have been given."

Love,
Grannie
xoxoxo

Several years ago, Pop and I were walking on the boardwalk in Ocean City. We started at the end and walked down to the beginning by Thrashers. On the return trip to get our car, we began to get tired. There was no choice but to continue if we wanted to get home. Pop found a rather large stone and kicked it to me. I returned the action to him. Soon we began our stone soccer game. Before long we were at our destination. We talked about how little by little, concentrating on the present moment, moving forward, we got to accomplish our goal. Soon we shared about the many other accomplishments we had reached in the same manner-without the stone.

It was two days before my 75th birthday. We took the same walk noting how many friends, due to their health, would not be able to experience this treat. Once again, as on most days, we shared how grateful we felt for all the gifts we had been given.

Why were we chosen to receive such gifts? We do not know. Yet, we work hard to use them to benefit ourselves, family, friends, and even strangers. We continue to discover these abilities and pray that each of you dear ones will do the same. Be patient with yourself. Trust yourself! And live with gratitude!

"Wear bright colors on raining days or days you just feel "POOPEY."

Love,
Grannie
xoxoxo

I attended Towson State College (now University) pursuing a lifelong dream of becoming a teacher. My reading class was one everyone looked forward to attending because of our wonderful, caring teacher.

One rainy morning, as he entered the classroom, our professor made the following comments. "I just love coming to this class. I especially love being with you on rainy days. My dear students, you always seem to wear bright colors at those times and that makes me feel happy."

I often think about his words and find myself putting on bright colors on a rainy day or a time period where I need an extra hug.

This little act, simple and silly as it may seem, does have a special way of adding sunshine and happiness to one's thoughts and day.

I always say to my children and often to others when circumstances are appropriate, "We know how to bring sunshine to our days…even if it is just wearing a colorful piece of clothing!"

"Every day, in some way, work towards getting and keeping your body healthy in mind, body, and spirit."

**Love,
Grannie
xoxoxo**

On the door of the Physical Education Department, there was this sign: "If you do not take care of your body, where will you live?"Another health related sign I recently read was "If you do not make time to stay fit, you will need to take time to go to the doctors."

Healthy eating, yoga, walking, working out in the gym, meditating, doing puzzles, playing cards and games, dancing, playing an instrument, being in stimulating positive company, drinking lots of water every day, taking supplements, and a good night sleep are just a few of the recommended ways to get and remain healthy. Take medicine only when it is really necessary. When having a medical concern, check it out by one in authority. Follow the treatment when needed. A little issue is much easier to take care of then trying to repair a major concern.

Some people will say good health comes from good genes, or it's just the luck of the Irish. From my life experience, I have not found those comments to be a 100 percent guarantee of good health.

Studies have proven that it is definitely an every day, lifelong commitment.

I pray that each of you will love yourselves enough and first to always do your best each day, in every way, to achieve this goal.

"Take time to listen to your inner voice."

Love,
Grannie
xoxoxo

One morning I was reading "Wrinkles Don't Hurt" –a daily positive quote about becoming older. This is a summation of that passage." We are all going to die sometime. We all do not know when. We all have things we want to do So…get started!"

It made me think of all the things I want to pursue. There are things I want to continue to do because I get great satisfaction from knowing I make a difference in someone's life-even if just on a tiny scale. I wish I would become disciplined to go back and take piano lessons again to enhance my much needed skills or even increase my expertise on gardening techniques. Many other things come to mind as well. My inner voice on this particular message stayed with me throughout the day.

At night, when all was dark and silent, I listened again to that soft inner voice and received another thought, "Bonnie Block, you are so lucky to have so many interests. You are also so fortunate to be able, in most cases, choose what you want to pursue. Take your time in moving forward."

Then I went to sleep peacefully, comfortable that I recognized my decision did not necessarily have a timeline-yet! Listening to my inner voice most often gives me a helpful pathway for creating solutions and exciting adventures.

"Eliminate, "I Can't" from your vocabulary."

Love,
Grannie
xoxoxo

There are so many times when our negative self talk or old rerun thoughts keep us from achieving a goal. This certainly can hinder our becoming all we can be. I presented an exercise to various populations on the theme of "I can't." In one of my kindergarten classes, children shared many things they believed they could not do. They copied the words "I can't "onto an index card and placed it in my big trash bag. We next walked to the cafeteria giving it to the custodian to dispose our paperwork. Getting back to our class, I expressed how we no longer had that word to say. Funny, how quickly the children adapted to this rule, even reminding someone who appeared to have forgotten.

I also presented this exercise to child care providers and parents. I did not know if it made a lasting impact on anyone. Yet, I do know that at the time of the presentations, I witnessed the positive effects of the participants' reactions.

When we say we can't, without even engaging in an attempt, that statement becomes the truth. When you think you can, you have a greater shot at "I am…"

"Have faith in a higher spirit, even when you have many unanswered questions."

Love,
Grannie
xoxoxo

My belief in a higher being came as a result of a very sad moment and of several special people on my life's journey. I always did believe in a God, but only as a passive part of my life. When I found myself praying, it was to my Daddy. To myself I'd cry," Daddy, please send me a sign you are with me." Believing he watched over me, something would happen, and I would feel he answered my prayer.

Teaching at Riverview, Karen, my school buddy, and I created and implemented many programs. She was deeply religious and openly talked about God. "Praise God! Thank you God!' she prayed aloud. I so admired her special relationship with her Lord. She became my religious teacher and enabled me to develop a very close relationship with my God.

Years later, another spiritual woman became part of my life. Sharon was my secretary and together we discussed life and God as our partner. I believe God chose to place those special women in my life to help me in my quest to build a meaningful relationship with Him.

Today, I feel comfortable to openly speak to God and talk about Him to others. I find myself thanking him aloud throughout my days. I never feel alone because I know God is with me. I do not question any more. For me, to have faith is not to seek answers.

My life is beautifully enriched because of my faith. I pray that each of you will develop a close relationship with a higher being. It is a gift of inner peace that you will give yourself forever. You will never feel alone.

"Remember when you A.S.K., you have a chance to G.E.T!"

**Love,
Grannie
xoxoxo**

Roger, my dear principal who gave me wings to fly, took me to a business partnership symposium. This was a new concept in our county. A wonderful gentleman from IBM sat with me for several hours denoting how such a program could have a major impact in my school. I left that meeting feeling so energized to pursue this new method for helping our children.

In the beginning of the new school year, I had just that opportunity. On our 25th wedding anniversary, at the Oneg Shabbat, I saw this successful caterer and well known philanthropist. Convincing myself this was the time to use my new skills, I traveled to where he was standing. "Thank you for all you do for education" I shared. From that comment, the following events developed. We met first to discuss the needs of our school. My principal and I then met with his board of directors. "Should we adopt this school?" he said. A gentleman, who lived by the school in his past, now his treasurer, said." YES!"

That was 27 years ago from this writing. Catered lunches, recognizing attendance, effort, citizenship, grades, various program supports, whatever was and is still needed, Uncle Marty and his team, have been and continue to be there for us. I could have never imagined all the blessings that were received just by A.S.K.ing!

"Listen carefully in order to really hear and fully understand."

Love,
Grannie
xoxoxo

In school I had been observing this child usually not listening to teacher's instructions. I also watched the girls in her class following her disrupted behavior. When the classroom door was opened, I could see the same pattern of behaviors existed. One day, the girl approached me and asked to come in my room for awhile. In our school, children seeming to need some time away often make this request. I gladly said," Yes" as I was happy to have time to discuss what I was observing.

We sat down together, and she began to share her many distraught feelings. She spoke about how she had always been the one who got in trouble since pre k, teachers did not like her, and then proceeded to explain about her family. Both parents were from other countries where many siblings still remained. She really was the one who had taken on all the responsibility for her younger and older brothers as well as helping her parents navigate this country. As I listened to her, I could hear her frustrations in most avenues of her young life.

I began listing all the ways I found her so very special and how the other girls in her class looked up to her. Sharing about how she could make a difference in the classroom, I next asked, "How can I help?" She responded," Maybe get the teachers together telling them we don't feel that they really care about us!"

I listened carefully to her remarks and heard how the feeling of" no one cares" permeated her entire conversation. I knew teachers in our school cared deeply, working hard to help their students reach personal and academic success. Obviously, this student had not received that belief. Now when seeing her, she will call out a hello, give me a high five, even a hug. I go out of my way to give her some indication of how much I truly care about her. I hope that message will eventually become one of her beliefs!

"Enthusiastically accept challenges and new adventures."

Love,
Grannie
xoxoxo

In 2000, congregants from Temple went to Israel. A side trip was to visit the Masada where a bar mitzvah was to be held. Most people get to the top of this religious site by cable car. My children, in their teens, climbed this mountain before and kept encouraging momma, "You can do it!" Seven people and yes, I was one, decided to engage in that challenge. Driving along the narrow roads to the site while looking up at those mountains, I kept thinking, "This looks like a movie. What in the world were those children thinking? What was I thinking?"

After sleeping (truthfully, just lying in a bed, wide awake, afraid that bugs or strange people would suddenly appear in our room) in this deplorable hostel, we met at 4:30 am. and began our journey upward. One person led us in prayer and as the sky continued to be midnight black, we began our climb. I was really doing great for awhile even though I often heard huffing and puffing from some of our troop.

Right before the last ¼ of a mile, I sat down and cried. I had never been so tired in my life. I heard, "Each man is on his own!" I knew they too were all pooped. I starting hearing my kids say," Mom, you can do it." I repeated that message til I finally arrived at the top! We all had a great story to share with the rest of the group when they arrived… by cable of course. From that time on, we called ourselves, "The Magnificent 7!" The bar mitzvah ceremony was awesome and the party after was amazing.

Some of the other unique adventures I have experienced were my mission trip to Cuba and volunteering in the Israeli Army with Pop when I retired from teaching.

When looking back on those special moments, I smile and just shake my head in amazement. I pray that Pop and I will be able to participate in many such adventures as we continue our awesome life's journey."

18

"Believe you already have all the courage you need."

Love,
Grannie
xoxoxo

Sometimes, I find myself doing an exciting, unusual activity and do not think about needing extra courage to become involved. I tend only to picture the greater part of the experience. It is not that fear doesn't exist for me. Rather, as Pop will often say, "I live in La La Land!" For me, that place feels safe and comfortable.

On one of our three visits to Israel (with many more to come I pray) this is what happened while praying at the wall. I was spit on and Pop was taken into a back room where they asked him for money as they prayed over him. I did need a little extra courage then. Then there was the time we volunteered in the Israeli Army and war broke out with Lebanon. Everyone from other areas was brought to our base for safety. We remained confined to our station all the while preparing supplies for war. I did need a lot of extra courage as I worried if I was ever going to see my children again. I had the opportunity to go on a mission visit to Cuba with my Temple bringing medical supplies to the poor Jewish community. When they stole some of our suitcase at the airport, my safe feeling did begin to change. When we were invited to attend a baseball game under strict orders of where to sit and never ever to leave the group, I did begin to question if living in La La Land in this opportunity was a wise adventure. Yet, thinking over such moments and others not shared, I realize I already had the extra courage, as in winning over my breast cancer. It seems during moments of necessity and after my first reaction, I find a way to go deep within myself and bring out the courage I have stored.

I pray that you will never need to call upon immense courage for some dreadful situation. Yet, believe that you will always be braver than you think and you will always have that courage you will need.

"Stop to admire the beauty of each season and be grateful you have the ability to see/hear their treasures."

Love,
Grannie
xoxoxo

♥ Pop and I often stop to admire the many beautiful and amazing gifts of nature. The colors, present in our environment, watching foliage that we (me really) planted from just a tiny little nothing and to see it blossom into a magnificent big something, makes us smile. Being able to feel and enjoy the different weather conditions, such as the sunshine, the cold, the snow and the heat, enhances our feeling of gratefulness.

In the spring and summer, when walking outside of my home in the morning, I often hear birds singing. I call them my little angels and share aloud, "Morning Angels, Thank you" and go on about my day. They too remind me of the wonder and majesty of God and how great life is!

At our beach condo, there are also many things that remind us of the wonder of our environment. From our sliding glass doors, we have a beautiful portrait of every season. We can observe the colorful changes in our beautiful surroundings, watch the ducks follow their leader as they travel across the pond, or glance up at the birds flying by in their v formation. With the addition of our fishing pond, an added gift has been given to us. People of all ages partake of this experience. Joy is an abundant feeling brought to all who engage in the activity as well as to those who choose to watch.

These are just a few of natures treasures that remind us of how fortunate we are to be alive and well, living in this great country, and observing such treasures.

"If looking for a significant other in your life, take all the time you need, and find one worthy of wonderful you."

Love,
Grannie
xoxoxo

♥ Pop and I lived in the same neighborhood and in 5th grade became childhood sweethearts. I was even his bar mitzvah date. We did like some other people at times. As I remember sharing with my mother, "I only had that special feeling with Alan."

In today's world, there are many ways, if one desires, to meet someone. Age is not even a factor if one is interested. I have heard senior citizens talk about writing notes or sending casseroles to those who have lost a spouse. Ugh! Oh I pray to God I am never in that position because Pop and I are living a very long, long healthy life together.

I really believe it is more important for a person to build a quality life dependent on his/her self. If someone comes along that you really care about, take time to get to know the person, and observe their actions in various situations, After your investigation, if you feel you have a match worthy of wonderful you, that's great…if that is what you want.

Just remember, it is not a race, you are not on anyone's time line. The quality of your choices equals the quality of your life.

Grannie thinks you are wonderful in every way and fully deserve to have all you want and of course only the best

"In all circumstances, always keep you personal power."

**Love,
Grannie**
xoxoxo

In the past, there were times when I had been in uncomfortable situations and times when I have felt less than for whatever reasons. I have been in a room where people would not give me a simple hello, want to talk to me, or even ask about the well being of my family. It was as if I was invisible while they continually talked about themselves.

In the past, there were times when I felt people were much smarter than me and oh so very worldly, having traveled extensively. There were times when I believed someone just wanted to hurt my feelings. I never once thought maybe they had the issue. Maybe they were jealous or just did not know how to be caring and nice. It was not a good feeling and at times had even caused me stomach issues. Often, I doubted myself just by others' remarks or actions. My faith in myself-well- I gave it away I guess from my own insecurity. Yep, in those types of circumstances, my personal power was nil.

Delores, our wonderful friend who made Thursdays so very special when she came to our home, gave me this wise advice. "In such situations, make out you are somewhere else."Many uncomfortable situations later, I was finally able to follow this sage's words. My cousin Sammy once shared, "When someone throws the ball at you (taking your personal power) either let it go by or catch it and quickly throw it back. Also, thru my meditations, I have learned other strategies to help overcome any uncomfortable feelings that just might arise.

Now that those experiences only lie way, way back underneath a heavy rock in my past and hopefully will never visit me again, I am indeed grateful for the above approaches and others I have acquired thru my faith and spiritual growth.

"Travel as often as you can, and of course, travel safe!"

**Love,
Grannie
xoxoxo**

♥ Pop and I have been most fortunate to travel to Israel three times and each was a different and most wonderful experience. The first time we went with people from many religious affiliations. The second was with members of our congregation. The third was to serve as volunteers in the Israeli army. Pop and I thoroughly checked out this program and they investigated us with the same intensity. Proud to say we passed with flying colors. To go was not an easy decision. Many kept sharing, "It is not safe. Do not go! What about your family?"

Pop and I talked endlessly as if to convince each other. We concluded that if we were to live life afraid to go anywhere and do many things we would be limiting the quality of our existence. The reality is that every day can have one or two segments that may be frightful or dangerous. Hence we decided to go and enjoy the moments.

We worked on the army base checking medical and ammunition supplies. At all times soldiers were always present. Every day, we ate with our protectors, and listened to many impressive speakers in the evening. Yes, their guns were always with them –even when off duty. At first sight of their ammunition, I must admit, I was frightened. I had never seen a gun up close. It did not take long before I realized it was just part of their uniform and their country's life style. Truthfully, as my children shared upon their return trips, and oh so many times, we repeated, you feel safer there than anywhere… perhaps even in your own home town.

Pop and I have traveled to many places, more than we could have ever imagined. Always we are aware of the excitement as well as the need to heed safety precautions. To be in Israel once let alone three times was only a dream. Now, we talk often, about returning to the homeland of our people.

"Take personal pride in all you do."

Love,
Grannie
xoxoxo

Loyola College invited me to teach people from Sudan and Eastern Europe how to become child care providers. My classroom was to be in the very back of this old resettlement center. It was a dark, messy small room with just a table that looked as if an animal had chewed several pieces out of the top. Upset by this learning environment, I found ways to make our classroom inviting. To brighten up our spot, I bought a flowered piece of material for the table. Each week I brought goodies to eat and things for themselves, their children and homes that I'd collected from family and friends. My activities were always meaningful, engaging and provided lots of fun. I had an interpreter that was one of the ladies' children, One day, I was presenting information about proper discipline procedures. I knew their countries had very strict rules, ones that we often think of as abuse. Giving each one a doll or stuffed animal, I began in detail, to explain what was considered appropriate. As the interpreter repeated my statements, the ladies seemed to have a lot to share on this topic. "What did they say?" I asked. My translator gave me a four word answer. We laughed both recognizing that was not the truth. At that moment, the walls of mistrust were broken down. They trusted me with their real feelings and I never wavered in my teaching for them.

After our first class, I hugged them goodbye and all left with a smile on their faces.. Before long, everyone was embracing each other and really feeling like a family. We even held a graduation party at our home where all the participants were beyond thrilled to get a school diploma!

Keeping my work ethics high, being the best Bonnie Block at all times, as well as my high, realistic expectations for my students, helped create this beloved and memorable family.

"Create a great team with your family and soul mate too."

Love,
Grannie
xoxoxo

I can picture Pop Block in the car with Grandma as they were leaving our home. As I stood by his car door, Pop looked me in the eye and shared, "Bonnie, you and Alan make a great team!"

Throughout our lives, Pop and I have done all we knew how to do at each moment to create such a team. Oh, there have been times when we were really mad at each other and the words flew around in a nasty flurry. More times than not, we worked diligently in each area of life, supporting and encouraging the other always.

Just as diligently and truthfully, even a little harder, we worked to always help our children feel loved, worthy and important. As a family, almost always, we went as one to school events, recreation activities, doctor appointments, movies, etc etc, etc. Sharing honest feelings along the way was a given.

One of the principles our team followed then and now is "Send In The Troops." Whenever one of our team members has been immersed in a good situation, I want everyone to recognize and celebrate with her or him. The same is true if one would need an extra hug for some type of worry or mishap. I quickly call the other members of our team to say," I need to send in the troops to …because……. They are then off to complete their assignment! I am most proud and grateful that being there for family is a life habit.

One of the greatest and most important ways I share with the children that they can honor Pop and I would be to always remain loving and supportive to each other, each and every day, in every way.

"Be the best "YOU" you can be in all situations and for certain, you will always be great!"

Love,
Grannie
xoxoxo

I was working with child care providers sharing different ideas how to enrich their after school programs. Some suggestions required extra time after hours. One participant shouted, "You get paid much more money than we do to put into the project!" I was a little taken back by her comments. Money has never been and remains not to be a motivating factor for doing my best in all situations. I responded. "Whenever I do something, I give 100 % of Bonnie Block to the task, completing my mission always to the best of my ability."

Thinking back on experiences I created or participated in, I always undertook them with intentions of giving my all to every project.

For example, I began Tiny Tots, an educational program when Michael was three, in the school where Barbie and Julie attended. Why would I not want to give time and energy if I did not plan to devote 100% of Bonnie Block to its implementation and success? I was a Girl Scout leader with my daughters and also one of their cheerleading coaches. Whatever it took to get the various tasks completed for its success, I was committed to doing.

I never have counted the hours when immersing myself in any activity or worthwhile adventure or experience. One thing that can be counted on, I always give my all, do my best. It really is a great feeling of satisfaction you derive from this discipline, even at a time when the project is not always as successful as you wished.

It is in the giving of yourself to such a project that even broadens who you are as a person and gets you ready for the next project.

"Be happy because something happened and let your tears be to a minimum because it's over."

Love,
Grannie
xoxoxo

♥ It was the school year 1992-1993. I was one of seven finalists for Maryland Teacher of the Year. I had been interviewed many times by a newspaper reporter and a local TV anchor. Cameras were often in my room. I was even asked to make a presentation the following morning after the gala. At the ceremony, I remember walking into this magnificent room with the other award winning nominees feeling so happy and proud. My whole family, the superintendent and school buddies were also in attendance. One of my sister's friends who was the event coordinator shared that my sister may want to attend this year's event! It was going to be special!

We walked onto the stage receiving congratulations from many Maryland leaders. Nancy Grasmick, State Superintendent, whispered in my ear," Just remember, you will always be teacher of the year." I smiled, we hugged and I took my seat waiting to hear the announcement of the winner. My name was not called and I remember everyone being very shocked as the tears just flowed from my eyes. It was upsetting as I was so encouraged by everyone that I just might be the State Teacher of the Year. Years later I found out that the governor called the organizers the night before. He exclaimed that a Baltimore county person could not win because they did not vote for him. Politics!

Whenever I hear someone share that aspect of my career, it feels a little embarrassing and at the same time, really nice. The thought of that experience does make me smile and feel so very proud that it even happened. I always felt like I won anyway because every day and to this very day I love that I am a TEACHER!

"It's where you are now that counts-NOW!"

Love,
Grannie
xoxoxo

Robert One lived in a poor neighborhood where many societal problems existed. His dedicated parents investigated how they could possibly help this terrific student attend an outstanding school to enhance his gifts. They found it! Robert attended an historic institution from middle to high school and became one of its outstanding leaders. He went on to college to become a teacher to help others obtain chances he was given. Today he is a terrific principal of a school similar to the population of his elementary school. I just know that many children will reach personal and academic success because of the angel at the helm of their schoolhouse. Lucky students, teachers, and parents!

Robert Two was a stay at home parent due to the expenses of a sitter. When both of his children were finally in school all day, he had a chance to pursue a career. I asked, "What would you like to do?" He answered, "I think to become a chef!" Because of our schools' partnership with the Maryland Food Bank and their wonderful educational program, Robert Two reached his goal! Today he is gainfully employed, has received several promotions, and is hoping one day to open his own pizza shop. He is so happy and proud of himself and rightfully so.

Robert Three was a foster child who lovingly slept on a cot in the dining room of a tiny row house occupied by 5 other people. He had some different learning abilities, had ups and downs in the business world, yet never stopped believing in himself. His positive attitude and constant willingness to help others aided him to become one of the most successful and happy persons in every way imaginable.

"Be a beacon of hope, joy, and love to someone, in some place, at some time, and with yourself always."

Love,
Grannie
xoxoxo

I was in the waiting area of the radiation department of Mercy Hospital. It was towards the end of my 39 weeks of treatment for breast cancer. Alan and I were sitting in chairs that faced into the room. Working on our Suduko puzzles, I noticed a woman and husband across from us. Her face expressed such despair, hopelessness and fright. Her feelings began to seep thru my body. I could recall one of the very first times I sat in this room with those same feelings. I found myself drawn to her pain. Before I knew it, I was out of my seat and sitting in the empty chair right next to her.

I began sharing how I could feel her thoughts and worries as I had been where she was now. Before long, I was telling her positive thoughts that others had shared with me to work thru this scary process.

All my actions, in that place, I believe, really came from a higher being. It was a call for me to cradle her with hope as others had done for me. In a soft, quiet voice, the couple expressed words of thanks over and over again. We became instant sorority sisters, even though our paths were never to cross again.

I went back to my seat, pencil in hand, planning to finish my puzzle. Instead, I reflected on how far I had come in my treatment, how far in my coming to terms with this disease, and how I really believed that I was going to be just fine! I was truly on the road to a complete recovery in mind, body, and spirit!

By my reaching out to that woman, I might have become a hero to her. For certain, I felt like, in that moment of time, a hero to myself as well!

"Take time to create a life you love."

Love,
Grannie
xoxoxo

It is Jan.4, 2018. Six days ago I celebrated my 75th birthday. It was a wonderful day. Part of my celebration was to spray my hair pink and ice skate with some of my grandchildren. As the year was ending and the new one was about to begin, I seemed to focus a lot on the things I wanted to do in the coming months.

Oh how grateful I am to continue to work at my Riverview School with my dear Mary M., one of my adopted daughters and my principal, and also my wonderful buddy and partner Mary P. We do not know about our positions for next year. Yet, I know for certain, it will be somewhere doing something to help make a difference. I thought about spiritual drumming, meditation, a class on wise aging, art classes, piano lessons, trips to New York, while continuing my yoga classes. So many exciting events… Maybe, just maybe, there could be a possibility I could do them all. Of course, any time I spend with my children and grandchildren brings an abundance of joy and blessings to enhance my very being. Each minute seeing or hearing about their daily lives makes me just smile even as I write these words on this paper.

As of this writing, I am happily participating in many of the above experiences. I have several planned New York trips to see Broadway plays. My most exciting one will be with my girls. This was a birthday present where we will go up to the city, spend time shopping of course, see a show and have dinner. The next day we will be in the audience of The View-my favorite show!!! Awesome and so very excited about that great, great present.

"Take your time Bon," is the message I often need to whisper in my ear. "Reflect on it all and then decide if YOU really love it!"

"Make time-as much as possible-to say to those you love, "I LOVE YOU!"

Love,
Grannie
xoxoxo

Growing up no one ever said what I believe are the most important words for anyone, especially a child, to hear from a parent, "I Love You!" The people in my world never gave a physical hug. No one even said good night when going to bed and or any other salutations during the day. I grew up keeping my thoughts to myself, never feeling anyone really cared about them anyway. Perhaps that is why at times I had been limited by the simple mantra I carried around with me, "I am not good enough."

I was lucky to have one wonderful angel in my life, my Granny Rose, Daddy's mom. When spending time with Granny(usually a very short span right after Sunday School) I felt loved by her dancing eyes, her compassionate smile, her loving words that she continually spoke to me and her physical hugs.

Loving Pop, and having Barbie Beth, Julie Carol, and Michael Brian and now Jordan, Yale, Ben, Ellie, and Nora made those word the most important sentiments I feel I could ever express to them. I truly adore them with all my heart and soul. Over the years I have taught myself how to express my love for them. Almost daily, when speaking with the children, I end with, "love you" and they share those sentiments back to me. Along with my words and actions, I choose to make" I love you" my life mantra. I have dedicated myself to sharing those sentiments to my loved ones as often as possible.

It is an eternal gift I get by having them in my life. I pray they will always remember and feel in their hearts how much Momma and Grannie loved them. I am beyond grateful that God chose to give them to Pop and I!

"Be present in the moment always."

Love,
Grannie
xoxoxo

My sister and I went to a meditation class at Hopewell Cancer Center. One day there was a most unusual presentation. Our teacher drew a large black V in the middle of a big sheet of white paper. "What do you see?" she asked.

We went around our semi circle giving many different responses. "A valley, a neckline, a bird, butterfly, a button" were just a few comments. As the last classmate spoke, I began to ponder the significance of such an exercise.

Finally, our leader shared. "I did not ask you to concentrate on just the black drawing. My question to you was what do you see? When you only concentrated on the drawing, you missed all the possibilities of the surrounding area."

Then she continued to share about our common disease. "If you are always focusing on the condition –all the what ifs-and on and on- you will miss all the whites that will surround you to enhance and bless your life."

I got the message! " Be Fully Present" in the moment you are currently living in. Be focused on the entire picture (your life) not just the one portion(the V).

This behavior will make challenges seem not so difficult while success will seem to come more often.

I pray dear ones, that you will always be fully focused in all the moments of your life.

"Recognize miracles (a good thing) regardless of size and be thankful."

Love,
Grannie
xoxoxo

♥ I believe that miracles happen all the time, all day long. I believe also that one just needs to look for and then label them as such. Also, I believe sharing them helps to bring more into one's life. Size is not a factor as to whether something can be so classified. I believe that this way of thinking is healthy for one's mind body and soul.

Here is a miracle that happened at the time of this first writing. There was a new program, Wise Aging, that I had hoped of taking this fall. Many places of worship were offering it. My temple was giving it on a day that I worked. I did not want to go to a night class. Another place of workshop was also offering it during the day and yet again, a time when I worked. However, the given time was later. If I could leave work a little earlier, I would be able to participate. I asked my principal if it would be possible to shorten my day to be able to attend such a program. Perhaps I could even bring something back to present to my parents. She said, "No problem!"

I was really excited about taking this class. The opportunity of meeting new people and having thought provoking opportunities were very motivating for me.

I successfully concluded this program and found it to be so very worthwhile. The group was to last for 6 weeks. Ours wanted to stay together and now we are in our 2nd year. I was even invited to work together with this national presenter on other innovative programs.

All because my principal said yes, I was able to participate in such a worthwhile program and make new wonderful friends. I call that, "A Miracle!"

"Believe God puts you where He/She needs you to be to help Him/Her do His/Her work."

Love,
Grannie
xoxoxo

Sonja was a beloved caregiver in our family programs. She was a parent of two boys, a school bus driver who worked her schedule to be part of our family of families, and was of the Muslim faith.

On this day, she attended class more than her usual quiet self. I greeted her with a warm embrace and asked, "Are you OK?" Sonja tightly hugged me back, holding that embrace a little longer than usual and sadly went to find a seat.

I began to think about the news I had heard in the morning while getting ready for school. It was then I began to understand Sonja's new behavior.

When the guest began to leave, I quietly asked her to stay back. Holding her hands in mine, I shared," I love you, you are a very special person, and that things are going to be all right. If you need to," I continued, "you could bring the boys and come stay with me."

Sonja tightly hugged me back and with tears in her eyes slowly stated, "Thank You"

I call that being a Merchant Of Hope! We are called upon at times when we do not know why or when. We just need to bring a ray of hope in to someone's life where there is a need.

"Surround yourself with positive people especially during difficult situations."

Love,
Grannie
xoxoxo

♥ Many times in life, uncomfortable and distressing things happen. When my friends learned of my health condition, everyone had the same response. "How can we help you?" One gift cancer gave me was learning how to say what I needed and not to feel less than because I wanted assistance. It took me a very long time to be able to give myself permission to respond in the following way…"I would love for you to just hug me-no questions, no comments, just a hug!"

Later, I was able to say, "Please only share positive things with me. I do not want to take a chance of putting any negativity into my body."

For some folks, this was a difficult request. They were use to retelling "stuff" and negativity was always filled in their stories., "Let me just finish this thought. This is not so negative" It was at that time when my opinion about the news was what was counted.

Today, I practice at being a cheerleader, sharing positive thoughts as much as possible to whomever I meet along my journey. At times, when I am in need of sending a get well card, I often choose to send a funny one denoting another time in someone's life…like a birthday, retirement, etc. I write, "I knew you were getting better and I just wanted to send you a hug and a smile."

The more I practice at being a cheerleader for others, the more I have become a cheerleader for myself.

"You will know you are making the correct choice by answering the question, "Is this choice true to who I am?"

Love,
Grannie
xoxoxo

❤ The brochure came from the senior center denoting a drumming class. I had experience with drumming in several spiritual arenas-once at an adult music camp where we drummed in the woods and once at a mediation class. I had tried a different class at this center before. The ambiance and the participants in the lecture did not fit with my personality. This class did sound interesting, Having loved playing drums in high school, having loved the piano and all music, I was ready to give the center a second chance. So many people really enjoy going there to attend classes.

The instructor began setting up the materials with big tall buckets that we placed huge balls on top. I had never had such equipment in my classes. Ok I thought, I will not make a fast judgment. Maybe this is something unique.

Escaping to the bathroom, I shared my horrific thoughts with Barbie about what was being offered. " Mom," she exclaimed, "you just went ice skating. What are you doing with all those old people? Get out of there!"

As I went back to the classroom, the teacher began instructing us to hold the ball and move from side to side. Then we were given drum sticks to hold over our heads and bring down to hit the balls in time to the music. I am thinking, "Yikes! This is not true to who I am! "The teacher could taste my feelings and said, "This is not what you are use to, is it?" I shook my head and thanked her for all she did to make a difference. Then I grabbed my purse and coat and I was out of there!

With all the things that I am doing and can do at this time of my life, thank you God, this was certainly not true to who "Bonnie Block" is currently!

36

"A smile can begin a relationship and always help to maintain one"

Love,
Grannie
xoxoxo

♥ I was outside gardening when a young woman got out of her car and came over to me. After greeting me with a beautiful smile, she asked," Do you need someone to help with the house chores?"

She proceeded to give me a neatly prepared handout denoting the many things she could do. She spoke in a pleasant tone the entire time, while continuing to keep that smile on her face.

"At this time, we have someone." I replied.

"That is ok." she said again in such a kind manner. "Perhaps you will keep my number in case things change."

"Certainly, I will do that!" and then she went back in the car and drove away.

I was thinking to myself," Boy, I wished I needed her services right now," She instantly made such a positive impression on me!

Before long, we did need someone-and yes-I found her paper.

Judy has been with me now for 12 years. She is truly an important member of our family.

It definitely was her smile and how nicely she spoke that made me save her information.

Yes, she is still smiling!

"Do your part in helping to break down walls of prejudice. One brick at a time is a good beginning."

Love,
Grannie
xoxoxo

♥ In kindergarten one year, I had a child who was a Jehovah's witness. In that belief, people didn't stand for pledging the flag. By the "WHAT" look on other children's faces, I decided to share my religious difference. The children were shocked to learn someone did not celebrate Christmas. That inspired me to share my holiday of Hanukah.

For several years, I held Hanukah celebrations in my room. A few times, Rabbi Berlin came to share details of how our holidays were different and alike. Even when the children moved on to other grades, they were invited to come back for the festivities. The audience consisted of parents one year. That celebration was then moved to the auditorium where we did Israeli dancing, sang songs and lit the menorah together. I believe all the children finally knew someone who did not celebrate their holiday and knew about the holiday she celebrated.

During one fall semester, I was teaching this college course and noticed that there was not any symbol for my holiday on campus. I approached the director to share this concern as many Jewish people attended that school. His response, "No problem. Bring in your holiday balls and we'll put them on the tree." I proceeded to share details of our celebration, and then he quickly left to find his secretary. "Please get a menorah to place under this tree" he asked. The ignorant response was, "A menorah? I thought that was what horses did!" When I returned to my class, I lividly shared what happened. "On the final exam will be what is a menorah and anyone who gets it incorrect, fails the class!" At the end of our session together, I received two gifts-really three. One was a children's Hanukah book, one was a handmade vest with dreidels all over it and one...the most important...everyone in the class knew the definition of a menorah!

"When someone says it's impossible, remember it is only their opinion."

Love,
Grannie
xoxoxo

♥ When I was growing up, girls whose families practiced Reform Judaism were not permitted to have a Bat Mitzvah. Boys had a Bar Mitzvah. Around the ages of 15-16, boys and girls were confirmed together in a joint service.

I was turning 60, and wanted to mark this significant time in my life in a very special way. Several weeks ago, I remember seeing a husband and wife read from Torah on our Bimah. I began to dream a little, 'Bonnie you could maybe have a Bat Mitzvah." When I shared this idea with my family, they responded "That would not be possible. Why not go on a trip?" Traveling is wonderful. However, at this moment in time I wanted to take part in something spiritual. Friends commented, "Are you kidding! Why? How? Forget it!" For me, that was not an answer.

I met with my Rabbi to share the wish. He stated, "It's a lot of work." and gave me a list of things I would need to do. "OK, I can do that!" For certain, no one really thought this would come to fruition, except me! I began to study Torah with a Hebrew scholar. "I will study with you. You can do this!" she exclaimed. Our Cantor helped me chant Troupe, the melody of the Hebrew words from the scripted Torah.

It was not easy. At one point, I remember being frustrated and most upset. Hysterically crying, I stated to Cantor, "Why did I do this? I cannot get this. Why did I even think I could do this!" She replied quickly and firmly, "You can! You will and you will be great!"

Well I did it! I was really great! We had a kiddish for everyone after the service and a disc jockey house party in the evening. It was beyond special and…not impossible!

"Always be opened to new possibilities."

Love,
Grannie
xoxoxo

As I am more than half way thru the writing of this book, two new possibilities of what kind of experience I would like to do next come to mind. One is that I am feeling inspired to write another book as I just love creating this project.

The second possibility, probably because Pop and I are now 75 and contemporaries have begun to downsize, we are thinking, "Is it time for us to move."

We do not have a first floor bedroom and thank goodness, we do not need it at this time, hopefully forever. Our home is in need of some repairs. Gratefully, we have the resources to fix them. Well….What do we do? Where would we go? Alan keeps asking, "Is there any place you would like to live?"

We checked out a community townhome with a first floor bedroom. We checked out a high rise building when the biggest unit became available. After seeing each, Pop and I both said, "They are not for us!"

When we arrived home, we sat and listed the multiple reasons we loved our home. They are in my journal dated sometime between April 7-9, 2018.

I always say God will show me what to do as He has always done. Just sometimes, I get a little impatient. Again, I just need to remind myself to quietly listen to my inner voice for the message.

Our plans for now have been finalized- to remain in our beautiful home, hopefully always!. When the time comes, and we want to move and or we need to move, we will be open to those possibilities.

"Find meaningful work that you enjoy doing, and then on most days, you will never really feel like you are working."

Love,
Grannie
xoxoxo

Since falling in love with my first grade teacher, Ms Burke, I always knew I wanted to become a teacher. After graduating high school and then Towson State, my dream became a reality. September 1965, my career as a teacher began. My first job was teaching first grade at Woodmoor Elementary School. After two years, I had my first wonderful child, Barbie and did not go back to teacher until Julie and Mike, my other two amazing kids, were older.

My next assignment was teaching kindergarten at Yorkwood and at Riverview Elementary Schools. After 7 years, I was invited to become an Assistant Principal at Colgate Elementary. Shortly after, I was offered another position that enhanced my life in ways I never could have imagined. I worked in the main office as the Child Care Provider for the entire county setting up programs and training providers. During this time, I presented workshops around the country at various seminars. It was during this time, that my popular workshop, "12 Ways To Hug Yourself" became published. Before retiring, I designed family involvement programs to help parents help themselves and their children reach personal and academic success. For the past 11 years, I worked again with wonderful families and the business community at the school I love-Riverview.

As I prepared to leave home each morning, I always said, "I am going to school." Rarely did I equate it as," ugh, going to work now."When in conversation about jobs, I always shared how much I loved what I do. Everyone always commented, "We can tell! Lucky You!"

How grateful I am to have been given the opportunity to choose the perfect profession for me! Dear children, I pray you can do the same.

"Being a good friend and choosing a good friend is a gift you give yourself."

Love,
Grannie
xoxoxo

Pop and I had many close friends in our neighborhood. After school and on weekends, we would all find ways to hang out with them-girls and girls, boys and boys and even boys and girls. A lot of us took dancing lessons together right in Frona's basement!

When Pop and I were first married, many young couples lived in the same area. One of Pop's dear friends, Abe, moved two doors down from our apartment after his marriage to Anita. It was there that our couple's friendship blossomed into something very special. "Uncle Abe" and ""Aunt Anita", Pop and I, did most things together. All five of our children felt so loved by each of the parents.

Aunt Anita had truly become my best friend, almost like a sister. We would call each other up many times during the day. Sometimes, it was just to say just a few words and our conversation would end

As of this writing, she has been gone 17 years and oh how I still miss her. I sure wish I could call her one more time and talk about life as it is today. I would love to share the great stories, (length not mattering) about my kids and grandkids and I could do the same about her babies.

We use to say that when we got old, we would be sitting on our rocking chairs saying, "Do you remember…" and we would smile and laugh at each thought. Just was not to be and that makes me feel sad even now.

Our friendship has never been duplicated. I recognize Aunt Anita was a very special gift that I had been given.

I will always be eternally grateful for our having chosen each other for a friend.

"Persevere, Persevere, Persevere!"

Love,
Grannie
xoxoxo

When Michael graduated from Lehigh, he wanted to work in New York. He sent out several of his great resumes but did not receive any job offers. Somewhat frustrated and of course disappointed, he came home to reevaluate his plans for employment.

Shortly after arriving home, Michael received a life changing phone call. It was a man from one of his dream companies that he had hopes of becoming part of their team.

"Michael, you have a wonderful resume. Unfortunately, we do not have any openings at this time. I will keep your paper work with me in case something turns up. My best advice I can share is Persevere, Persevere, Persevere!"

The very next day, Michael decided to go back up to New York. He now brought with him, besides his resume, a new positive outlook on his job hunt. It was not long after, that Michael obtained his goal-a New York job!

That mantra has been one that has been adopted by many in our family as we sought ways for pursuing many dreams.

Remember, "Every day is a chance to begin again and/or dream something new."

"There is no time limit in discovering all your gifts."

Love,
Grannie
xoxoxo

- Attend an eight day conference in California by myself-WHAT???
- Flying across the country by myself to present workshops in different places in the USA-What?????
- Participating in the Polar Bear Swim in January-WHAT?????
- Climbing Masada –WHAT?????
- Reading from the Torah at Yom Kippur morning services-WHAT?????
- Becoming a Bat Mitzvah at 60-WHAT?????
- Driving to the beach by myself-WHAT?????
- Staying at home, in a hotel, or at the beach by myself-WHAT?????
- Becoming a published author, at any time yet alone at 70-WHAT?????
- Writing a second book-WHAT???
- Becoming a Minister and officiating at weddings-two being my former students-WHAT?????
- Being invited to develop a women's group with Muslim and Jewish women-WHAT????? AND…….who knows what I will be doing next (probably forgot some in this category) I wonder what other gifts I have that have not been discovered. I am excited to see when they will appear and where they will take me. HMMMM

This following thought I based my bat mitzvah sermon on. It continues to bring me joy and peace

"Rejoice in the past. Engage in the present. Delight in the future"

"Create positive affirmations
to read daily."

Love,
Grannie
xoxoxo

♥ I had the wonderful opportunity to attend two Facilitating Self Esteem Seminars led by Jack Canfield in California. Each conference lasted for eight days and became a personal self awareness investigation. We understood we needed to complete the exercises in order to help others do the same.

During the second conference, participants became aware of the significance of personal affirmations and how to create them. An affirmation is a positive statement, written with a feeling word, in the present tense, as if it already happened. "I am gratefully rejoicing now that I am helping to make a positive difference every day in any way." is one of mine.

I wrote several during the sessions and have continued to create them ever since. I write them on 5 by 7 colored index cards and place them in a fancy binder. They relate to all aspects of my life.

"I am gratefully rejoicing now that Alan and I, Barbie, Julie, Mike, Adam, Tracy, Bobby, Jordan, Yale, Benjamin, Ellie and Nora 's bodies are always healthy physically and emotionally every day, in every way, all thru their very long, long, long, long, long lives.

I read the statements almost every morning. They have become a personal prayer book of sorts. I have created them with family in mind, and at times, in regards to the needs of friends and even strangers.

A prayer list for those in need of healing, in some fashion is also included.

It is a very sacred and special text for me that always continues to bring me peace as well as hope.

"Having a happy heart enhances everything."

Love,
Grannie
xoxoxo

Riverview Elementary School will hold their annual talent show and I will be again one of the chairpersons along with assistance from Mary P and other staff. I just know it will be another fun time for everyone. The children get so very excited to participate. Many times throughout the beginning of the year, they will ask, "Ms Block, When is the talent show?" It is indeed a happy memory for everyone.

The acts are developed entirely by the students and at times by the aid of older siblings, teachers and /or parents. In all the years I have been involved with this program, only one child had been professionally trained. However, our boys and girls beam with confidence as they become STARS.

Everyone who tries out does get to be involved. The excitement continues to build from the first announcements, to when the flyers go home, and during the many conversations of the want to be participants in regards to their performance.

This happiness stays thru the entire talent show and really thru most of the rest of the school year. The STARS become like a family, cheering others on to success. They often greet each other when seeing "The STARS" in the schoolhouse.

An added positive impact from this activity is that behavior problems are down as to be in the show they can only exhibit STAR behavior.

Happiness is an inside job. We, on the outside, can help those find happiness even if it is just for one morning at school.

"Treat yourself with loving kindness, compassion, and acceptance of where you currently are and be with peace."

Love,
Grannie
xoxoxo

I had turned 75 in December. We spent the following June, July and August living in our beach home. What a blessing! It feels like a pinch me miracle even now as I write my thoughts on this topic.

During many quiet moments, looking at the ocean, or walking along the beautiful paths, I began reflecting as to where I was on my life's journey. How was aging going to affect my life? What gifts could it bring? What limitations/challenges might it also present? I knew I wanted to engage or continue participating in many activities to stimulate my mind, body and spirit. What to do? How do I make decisions that seemed to not have the regular boundaries as when I was younger? Sharing this dilemma with a young person, he immediately exclaimed, "Why not do them all?"

I remember a time sharing with one of my children, "I feel like a jack of all trades, master of none." The quick reply was, "Which one would you give up to master another?" "NONE!" I firmly stated. "There's your answer!"

It was at that moment I began to feel at peace in the exploration. I started to treat myself with kindness and compassion along this ambitious adventure, giving myself positive messages when needed.

"According to the effort is the reward."

Love,
Grannie
xoxoxo

Celebrating holidays with family and dear friends has been a wonderful tradition in our home. Why, we can seat 29/30 people and buffet is limitless! Alan and I work very hard to make certain all the details are worked out before our guests arrive.

Pop does most of the cooking as he is a really good cook. Our children and guests always offer to bring something to add to the delicious meal.

I plan and facilitate the sacred moments and entertainment. Before holiday dinners, I create a mini sermon based on what is happening in our lives. Always I conclude with an uplifting, positive thought. When dinner is over, the children take part in a mini play of sorts that I have written. The audience participates as well.

All the festivities are a lot of fun and yes, we will admit, a lot of work. The rewards, oh the many rewards, are just beyond measureable.

Truly, Pop and I try hard to create such quality times with each other, our children and their families that will hopefully stay in their hearts forever.

"Making memories is a gift you give yourself!"

"A loving family is made up of trillions or more tiny memorable moments."

Love,
Grannie
xoxoxo

We really did most things as a family-Pop and I, Barbie, Julie and Michael. It was always understood that we were a team. School events and other activities, even doctor appointments, we all went together as a family. We ate dinner together, each one having "stuff" to share. If one person had an after school activity, we waited til everyone was able to be seated at the dinner table.

During tax season, we tried our best to wait for Pop to come home. If we were hungry and a snack did not do the trick, we would have our evening meal. Yet, later, when Pop arrived home, we all sat at the table and gave him updated details of the day.

We had a TV in the family room and a little one in our bedroom. With dinner, homework, and baths completed, we all sat bundled up with cozy blankets, on our cozy sofa, eating popcorn and watching a show we all decided on together. We were all happy to be part of the Team Block Family.

Hearing Barbie, Julie and Michael recall stories of the trillions of times, whether in the past or present, when we were all together.("Do you remember when…"and it can go on and on and on…) is an eternal hug I receive just from listening.

I always share that the greatest legacy Barbie Beth, Julie Carol, and Michael Brian can give to Pop and I is always remaining loving and supportive to one another every day, in every way. In my heart, I truly believe that this will always, always, occur.

Creating family is a full time, lifelong job. The rewards are beyond the language I have to express!

"Always remember, everyone had to start somewhere."

Love
Grannie
xoxoxo

♥ Should I adventure into taking an art class? I met a friend who shared the class she was taking. She mentioned how esteeming the professor was to everyone, regardless of ability. I knew replaying tapes of being good enough would likely have me pass this opportunity. I kept thinking about this conversation and silently saying," Bon, those old messages are really silly. Ok, I will at try it." I signed up for the local college senior art class. This experience taught me to see that I had the power to change my thoughts, any time, in any situation.

As I took my seat in class, I noticed the masterpieces of the other students. I was not ready to instantly drop out, but I did think I would do it at the end of the period. My first assignment was to draw and paint a lily. I eventually began to create. Shortly thereafter, my professor came to view my attempts. I whispered "This is my very first time I have done something like this." He gently shared, "That's ok! Everyone had to start somewhere." Quietly, he walked away. Silently, I repeated what would soon become my new mantra, "Everyone had to start somewhere." That sentiment kept me moving forward and I completed all five assignments. The last one, the rose, was my proudest masterpiece and is hanging in my office.

Gratefully, I share, that many of my old limiting tapes are disappearing as I continue to work on dismantling several others. Oh, how I wish I could have been able to have that belief when I was much younger. Once again I realize, that every new day is a chance to begin again, dream anew, and try something unique.

I pray you will always have the courage, and love yourself unconditionally, without having limiting tapes, to engage in the future in any way you choose. (and to help others do the same)

"Bigger is not necessarily better."

Love
Grannie
xoxoxo

In the evening, when everyone's rituals were completed-homework, dishes, pajamas on, etc, we all met in our den to spend the remaining of the evening together. With only one TV for all to share, the family had to compromise as to what was going to be watched. I am proud to share that this was not a skill that was a problem for the Block family.

Let's fast forward. We are beginning out 8th year, at our wonderful beach condo in Bethany Beach. Once again, for our family, the act of compromising was necessary. There are three bedrooms, one being ours. When two families want to come down together, everyone must figure out where to sleep. They work it out- each one choosing a special place for their bags, toothbrushes and of course, their bodies at night. As a parent, I love watching this occur, and of course, cherish, that as many as possible are visiting us at the same time. Playing games, being at the beach, having a meal, or just sharing current thoughts and or stories from long ago, it feels like a magical time. It often reminds me when they were just little people. Oh how proud I am of each and every one. They are indeed such fine human beings.

This summer I am extra excited because Pop is getting another place for a week so everyone can be together -all our children and grandchildren together. I am so looking forward to sharing such special moments.

In today's big world, being in a sort of family nest once in awhile, for me is a blessing. Those times I believe, deepens the meaning of family.

Pop and I are so very blessed to have all of them in our lives. So grateful!-Thank you God!

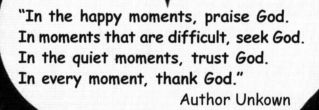

"In the happy moments, praise God.
In moments that are difficult, seek God.
In the quiet moments, trust God.
In every moment, thank God."
                              Author Unkown

        Love,
        Grannie
        xoxoxo

"New Messages"

Printed in the United States
By Bookmasters